*When God's mercy
is too hard to swallow*

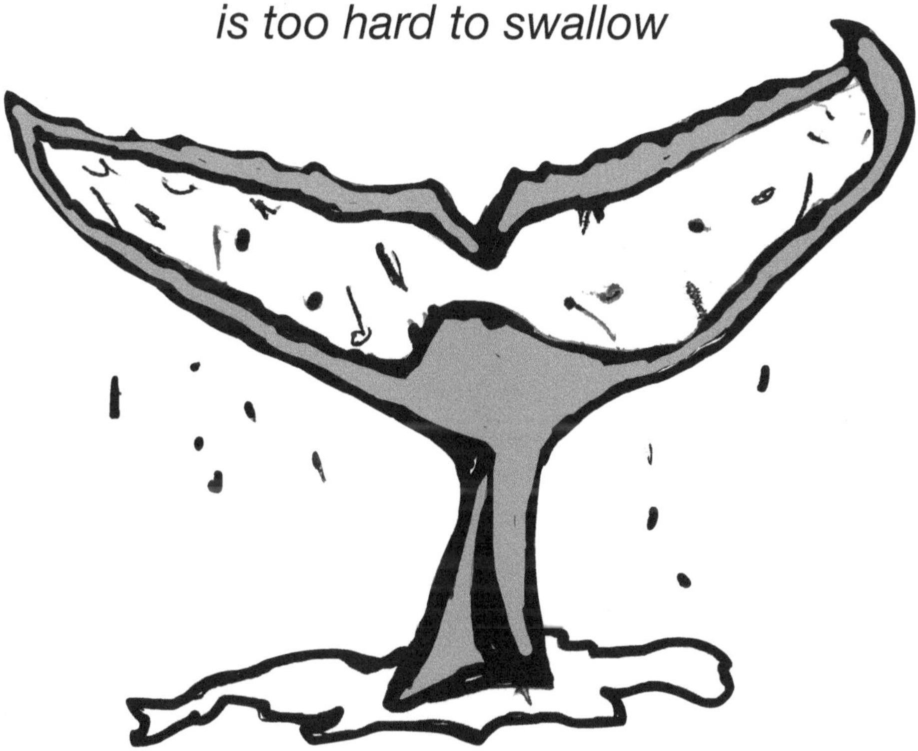

The Little Bird Bible

Jonah

Retweeted

Jarrod Branson Conyers

Little Bird Bible Jonah Retweeted
Copyright 2022 by Little Bird Bible LLC
All Rights Reserved.

No part of this publication may be reproduced, stored in a retrieval system or transmitted, in any form or by any means electronic, mechanical, photocopying, recording or otherwise, without prior written permission from the publisher, except for the inclusion of brief quotations in a review. All images are also under the same copyright limitations.

All characters real, historic, or imagined may have no knowledge or concept of the Little Bird Bible
and thus do not endorse it.

For information about this title or to order other books and/or electronic media, contact the publisher.

ISBN: 978-1-7335122-5-1

Printed in the United States of America
Cover and Interior design: Little Bird Bible LLC.

Dedication:
To every one of us
who has been through the belly of a whale
and lived to tell about it.

Special Thanks To:
Dr. Regina Hunter
and
Dr. Stewart Lasine

for their guidance and scholarship
with this unique undertaking

Jonah Retweeted — vii

Foreword — vii
- What Is Little Bird Bible? — vii
- What Makes The Little Bird Bible Different? — vii
- E-Reader Sticker Bonus — x
- Try Little Bird Bible Abridged — x
- Other Key Features — xi

The Backstory of Jonah — 1
- The Author — 1
- The Book — 1
- The Audience — 2
- The Key Places — 3

Chapter 1 — 5
- Chapter Breakdown — 5
- Chapter 1 Emoji Lexicon — 6
- Chapter 1 & Comment Threads — 7
- Chapter 1 Reflection & Discussion — 16

Chapter 2 — 19
- Chapter Breakdown — 19
- Chapter 2 Emoji Lexicon — 20
- Chapter 2 & Comment Threads — 21
- Chapter 2 Reflection & Discussion — 27

Chapter 3 — 31
- Chapter Breakdown — 31
- Chapter 3 Emoji Lexicon — 32
- Chapter 3 & Comment Threads — 33
- Chapter 3 Reflection & Discussion — 40

Chapter 4	**43**
Chapter Breakdown	43
Chapter 4 Emoji Lexicon	44
Chapter 4 & Comment Threads	45
Chapter 4 Reflection & Discussion	53
Jonah in Short	**57**
Pictorial Character Directory	**58**
Endnotes	**75**
Author Bio	**77**
What's Next for LBB?	**78**

Jonah Retweeted

Foreword

What Is Little Bird Bible?
Every day billions and billions of text messages and social media posts containing emojis are sent expressing the thoughts and feelings of people across the world in short, succinct ways, but thus far, this modern and global form of communication remains independent from the message of Holy Scripture, which we believe is also meant for all people. Thus, the idea of translating a new condensed paraphrase of the Bible using emojis and formatted within the parameters of social media came to be, and the Little Bird Bible was hatched with the mission **to simplify and enhance the Bible reading experience for 21-Century audiences.** The Spirit of God descending from heaven like a dove, as described in John 1:32, is the image and metaphor we use in our books in the hopes that your mind, imagination, and faith will similarly be inspired from on high.

What Makes The Little Bird Bible Different?

1. Illustrative language
Instead of creating a *literal equivalent translation* of the Bible, which strives to accurately translate the prose, syntax, and words of Scripture from their original languages, The Little Bird Bible is a new type of *dynamic equivalent translation*. It seeks to capture the thoughts and feelings 🤗 🤢 🥺 😬 of the original authors with the pictorial language of emojis and stickers. Thus, this Bible is not a replacement for traditional translations; it is a supplement for the devoted and the curious when reading their own preferred Bible translation.

What is more, even though emojis are used universally around the world through a specific, ever-expanding font called Unicode (Currently version 15), there is disagreement about what some emojis mean. There are also many words and ideas for which no singular emoji currently exists, so The Little Bird Bible often combines several emojis to create an idea or concept. To help define and reveal the meaning of these unique emoji combinations, we also use background colors and an emoji lexicon to assist the reader.

Background Colors. The emojis used in a sequence are set on a unifying background-color block to help you interpret their compound meaning:
Tan = General,
Purple = Holy,
Black = Dark,
Red = Sinful

Chapter Lexicons. At the start of each chapter, a reference guide lays out in sequential order the key emojis and unique emoji combination as they are used for the first time in that chapter alongside their intended definitions. Emojis used in their literal or common sense are not included.

2. Perpetuating Dialogue
The Bible is often treated as a static, historic, closed, divine offering, instead of as a progressive and expanding dialogue of God's revelation to the world, so we are hopeful that every edition of the Little Bird Bible gives you, the reader, an opportunity to engage, debate, and discuss the text as well. To help facilitate this dynamic, this *Retweeted Version* of the book adds a number of comment threads indented throughout the main text. These comments are voiced by a theologically diverse cast of famous, historic, and sometimes imagined characters across time; we hope their debate and discussion of the original text from their unique

faith perspectives will help you, the reader, learn about many key people in our faith history and broaden our collective theological understanding.

We hope you will continue the conversation online with your own understanding and interpretation of the text, so within each chapter, the Little Bird Bible provides a series of hashtag prompts (i.e. **#newleaf, #divinepatience**) to post on your favorite social media platforms.

3. Emotive Icons and Stickers
Where many contemporary Bible translations employ the use of religious art and icons, the Little Bird Bible takes this to the next level by introducing inline iconography; every passage of scripture is written alongside the colorful image of the individual that is speaking, writing, or quoting it. This unique inline iconography helps identify and clarify what is being said while underscoring the emotion of the text; the face of each icon changes to reflect their mood from passage to passage in addition to their age as time passes. The usage of these simple icons also creates a unifying stylized depiction of Biblical people that spans both Old and New Testaments with the intent of bringing greater harmony between them. The same stylistic approach is used for other non-Biblical characters that take part in the retweeted side conversations. To help familiarize the reader with the cast of characters, at the back of each *Retweeted Version*, you will find a special Pictorial Character Directory containing a brief biography of each person. In addition, the color of the border surrounding each character's icon, is designed to help the reader instantly and visually classify what each character's primary category is.

There are eight character categories and eight matching border colors:
1. Royal Blue: Old Testament people
2. Aqua Blue: New Testament people

3. Red: Philosophers & Theologians
4. Green: Inventors & Scientists
5. Grey: Antagonists & Critics
6. Yellow: Musicians & Artists
7. Purple: Spiritual Beings
8. Brown: Leaders & Experts

A white star indicates the character reflects a generic viewpoint but does not embody an actual person.

E-Reader Sticker Bonus

THANK YOU FOR CHOOSING THIS PRINT VERSION OF THIS LITTLE BIRD BIBLE BOOK. MANY OF OUR ICONS ARE ORIGINALLY FORMATTED AS DIGITAL STICKERS. IF IN THE FUTURE YOU PURCHASE A DIGITAL VERSION OF ANY OF OUR BOOKS, AND IF YOUR E-READER SUPPORTS GIF FILES, YOU WILL SEE THEM COME TO LIFE. THESE ANIMATED STICKERS ADD AN EXTRA LAYER OF EMOTION BEHIND THE TEXT AND AN ADDED ELEMENT OF FUN WHEN READING THE BIBLE THAT TRADITIONAL PRINT FORMATS CANNOT EXPRESS.

4. Living Footnotes

Where many Bible translations use tiny numeric footnotes to further elaborate on textual variations or historical context, the Little Bird Bible uses the side conversation dialogues to do the same thing in a more dynamic way. The dialogues provide concordance references to other Biblical passages, identify thematic and scriptural parallels, expand the historical context, and reinforce the theological value of your Bible reading experience.

Try Little Bird Bible Abridged

It is possible that you may find the side conversations and living footnotes distracting and that they keep you from enjoying this unique emoji translation of the Bible. If that is so, then please discover the *Abridged Versions* of many, but not all, Little Bird Bible books. The *Abridged Versions* use the same dynamic equivalent emoji translation of the Bible in a straight forward uninterrupted format, yet they also retain the relevant emotive icons of the New and Old Testament figures to more clearly identify who is speaking in the text. What you get is an even shorter, modern, sleek Bible translation that is more concise and focused.

Other Key Features
Every Little Bird Bible book employs a number of additional features that we you hope you will enjoy, such as
In-line Pronunciation Guides with difficult names, **Chapter Breakdowns** of what lies ahead, **140-Character Count Chapter Summaries** of what you just read, **Discussion & Reflection Questions** to connect with the text, and **Gender-Inclusive Language** for all people.

Thank you for choosing this Little Bird Bible book. I hope this and future LBB books will serve to kindle your imagination, challenge your own interpretation of Scripture, and provoke or establish a devotional life that connects you in a meaningful way to God.

To Him Be the Glory 🐦🎼🙏!

J.B.C.

The Backstory of Jonah

The Author
The book of Jonah is named after the minor Old Testament prophet of the same name who provides an intimate first-person account of the action. However, the story reads as a third-person narrative; thus, the LBB story of Jonah will be told by the LBB Narrator to remain consistent with the storytelling and better reveal the moments when Jonah speaks for himself. A prophet named Jonah son of Amittai is also first mentioned in the book of 2 Kings 14:25, where he prophesies that King Jeroboam II of Israel will expand his kingdom. Many scholars assume they are the same person, and if so, this sets up a paradox before the book of Jonah even begins. While speaking on behalf of God in favor of a bountiful future for their leader and their nation no doubt made Jonah well-known and popular, God then calls him to prophesy to the capital city of Israel's greatest enemy (Assyria). This makes Jonah angry and spiteful. Most of what happens in the book does not reflect well on Jonah, and he may have been reluctant to share his journey, however, one of the major points of this story is to show the measures God will take to accomplish His purpose in spite of the flawed messengers He sends in His name.

Jonah

Narrator

The Book
Most people often and only associate Jonah being swallowed by a whale, but the book uses this only as a small part of the larger narrative that describes God's expansive dominion and mercy. The date of its writing is hard to pin down given that there are very few internal time stamps; most scholars date the book between 843-793BC based on when Jeroboam II and when the assumed King of Assyria reigned; others suggest the date of the writing and the story's historic setting are not the same.

The book of Jonah is only four chapters long, but they are carefully written so that the first two chapters and the last two chapters follow a similar arch: 1. Jonah is told to preach to Nineveh, 2. Jonah encounters non-Jewish peoples in trouble, 3. These outsiders turn, confess, and believe in Jonah's God, 4. Jonah subsequently pouts. As you read, watch for the contrasts and paradoxes poignantly written into the story.

The Audience

Even though Jonah's message from God was directed toward the people of the Assyrian capital of Nineveh, the message of the story was given to the broken and destitute people of Israel, who based on the time period of the book's writing were either just conquered by Assyria, were being conquered by Assyria, or were about to be conquered by Assyria. What we gain from history is that "the Assyrians were a cruel and heartless people who thought nothing of burying their enemies alive, skinning them alive, or impaling them on sharp poles under the hot sun."[1] Given that context, the very idea that God would be willing and wanting to forgive Israel's greatest enemy was probably received as being both offensive and ridiculous. If the Almighty is willing to do such a thing, then can his followers really refuse to do the same thing? Thus, the book is the only book of the Bible that ends its story by asking its intended audience such a question.

The Key Places

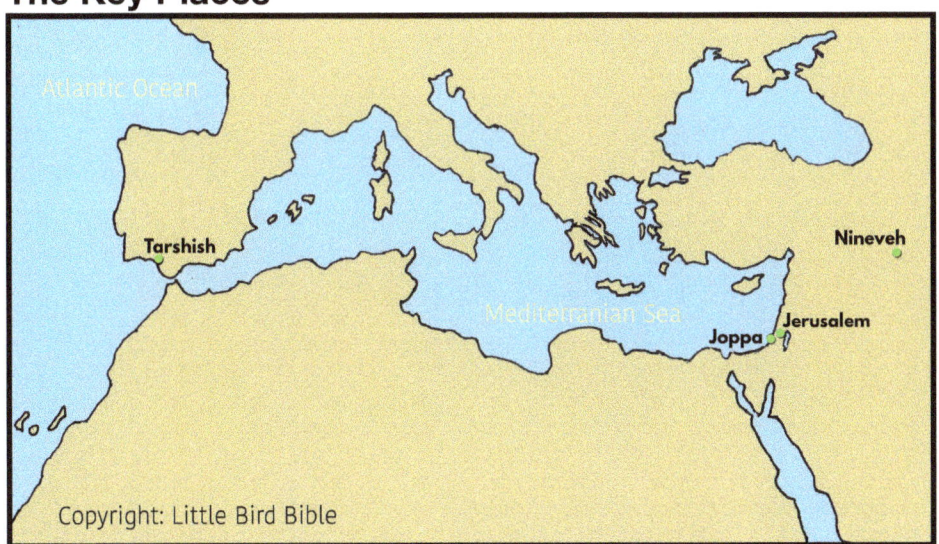

We know the historic locations of Nineveh, Jerusalem, and Joppa; Tarshish, however, is unclear. While Jonah flees to Tarshish in the opening sequence, the exact location of this place is debated by many scholars, as it could mean a generic place that is unimaginably far away, as we might describe going to "Timbuktu." Timbuktu actually is a real physical place, and many scholars argue the same about Tarshish. The most convincing argument suggests that it is off the Coast of Spain near modern day city of Tarifa. Wherever it was, the point is that it was in the exact opposite direction of Nineveh, and it was very far away.

Chapter 1
Chapter Breakdown

Verses 1:1-3
The Lord God gives Jonah a message to deliver to Nineveh, the capital of one of Israel's greatest enemies, but Jonah refuses to deliver it and gets on a ship going in the opposite direction.

Verses 1:4-7
Jonah falls asleep aboard the ship and is unaware that God has sent a great storm to keep him from running away. The ship is reckoned to sink, so the terrified sailors lighten the load, pray to their gods, and then discern that Jonah is responsible for the calamity.

Verses 1:8-12
As the storm gets worse, Jonah tells the ship's crew that he is a prophet of the Most High God and that he alone is responsible for the tempest; Jonah suggests the crew throw him overboard so the storm will subside.

Verses 1:13-16
After trying all they could to avoid Jonah's suggestion, the crew prays to Jonah's God to not be angry with them for tossing the prophet overboard. Once they do, the sea becomes dead calm and they worship the Most High God.

Verse 1:17
The Lord God provides a great fish that swallows Jonah as he sinks.

Chapter 1 Emoji Lexicon
The sequential usage & definitions of non-literal emoji concepts

Jonah 1:1-3
😇🧑‍🏫📣 =Prophet
🏢🏛️🕰️ =City
📞 =Call
👹 =Wicked
🏃🔙 =Run, Ran

Jonah 1:4-7
🌬️ =Wind
🌊 =Sea
🙏 =Pray
⬅️👀 =See, Look
🤔💭 =Remember
💀 =Die, Dying

Jonah 1:8-12
👨‍👩‍👧🚩 =Tribe
✡️ =Jew
🇮🇱 =Israel
🐝🍁 =Believe
⛅🌌 =Heaven
😌⬇️ =Calm Down

Jonah 1:13-17
😇 =Holy, Pure
👍 =Good
ℹ️ =Revere
🐑🗡️ =Sacrifice
✋📖 =Vows
🌅 =Days
🌃 =Nights

The Book of Jonah
Chapter 1 & Comment Threads

Jonah 1:1-3

Narrator @TheDivineWord
A long time ago, the Lord spoke 💬 this message to Jonah the prophet 😇🧑‍🏫📣:

God @TheLivingPresence777
"Get ⬆️ & Go to the great city 🏙️🏛️🏢 of Nineveh (NIN-uh-vuh) & 📞 out against it 😫, because its wickedness 👹 has come ⬆️ before me."

>
> **Prof. Rosenbaum** @HebrewScholar7
> *This is a very common way to start the account of a prophet: **Joel 1:1, Micah 1:1**, and **Jeremiah 1:4** all begin the same way with God proclaiming his message to his messenger, but Jonah is the only one who doesn't deliver it.*

Narrator @TheDivineWord
But Jonah ran 🏃 ⏪ away from the Lord & headed for Tarshish (TAHR-sheesh). He went ⬇️ to Joppa (JAHP-uh), where he found a 🚢 bound for that port. He bought a 🎟️, went aboard, & sailed ⛵ for Tarshish to run 🏃 ⏪ from the Lord.

>
> **Prof. Lui** @GeographyGuru
> *It is worth noting that Tarshish was in the exact opposite geographical direction than Nineveh was and several thousand miles farther away.*

Prof. Rosenbaum @HebrewScholar7
*More to the point, the Hebrew text clearly points out that Jonah was not running away from Nineveh or his responsibility, but the "face of God" not once, but twice, in **verse 1:3**.*

Father Mapple @MobyDickPreacher
"Jonah sought to flee worldwide from God? Miserable man! Oh! most contemptible and worthy of all scorn; with slouched hat and guilty eye, skulking from his God; prowling among the shipping like a vile burglar hastening to cross the seas."[2]

Adam @TheVeryFirstMan
*I also hid from the face of God (**Genesis 3:8**); I don't recommend it; He will always find you.*

Prof. Winglethrush @LiteratureIsLife
Thus surmised Francis Thompson in his famous poem,"<u>The Hound of Heaven</u>;" Divine Grace will follow and hunt down every distant soul until it is forced to turn to God alone.

Jarrod @LittleBirdBible
It sounds like the great Hound of Heaven is always pursuing us even in the midst of our pain and suffering, yet feeling abandoned by God in the midst of pain and suffering is a pretty common complaint people make. Where is the line between Divine Abandonment and Holy Pursuit?

What do you think? Post about it:
#HoundofHeaven

Login: <u>Facebook</u>; <u>Instagram</u>; <u>Twitter</u>

Jonah 1:4-7

Narrator @TheDivineWord

Then the Lord threw a great wind 💨 on the sea 🌊, & such a violent storm arose that the 🚤 threatened to break ⬆️. All the sailors were afraid 😨 & each prayed 🙏 hard to his own god. They threw the cargo into the 😠🌊 to lighten the 🚤.

But Jonah had gone ⬇️ below deck, went to 🛏️, & fell deeply into 😪. The captain went to him & said,

Captain @TarshishBound

"Get ⬆️! 📞 on your god! How can you sleep ❓ Perhaps he will look ⬅️👀 & remember 🤔💭 us, & we will not die 💀."

Mark @TheFirstEvangelist
*That's funny; I remember something very similar happened to the 12 Disciples, when Jesus went below deck and fell asleep. (**Mark 4:35-41**)*

Paul @WorstSinnerEver
*I can relate; a very similar disaster occurred to Luke and me as we sailed to Rome for my trial before Caesar. (**Acts 27:13–44**)*

1st Mate @TarshishBound

"Hey guys, let's roll 🎲🎲 to figure out who the guilty person is so we can 👉 blame 👈 them for this calamity 😩 we are in."

Narrator @TheDivineWord
So, they rolled 🎲🎲, & the 🎲🎲 fell on Jonah.

Prof. Storia @HistoryIsLife
Ok, they did not roll dice; they "cast lots." This was an ancient form of divination to determine God's will where two stones (the Urim and Thummim) were used and the outcome was predicated by chance.

Jarrod @LittleBirdBible
Oh, you mean like how we use dice?

Hellen @OffendedLayPerson
I am offended you are suggesting the Bible promotes gambling!

Prof. Storia @HistoryIsLife
*It's not gambling. The Ancients used these stones to decide complicated issues in an impartial and fair manner under divine influence—not to get rich fast. Plus, they gave God the credit (**Proverbs 16:33**).*

Einstein @E=MCSquared
"God does not play dice."[3]

Jonah 1:8-10

2nd Mate @TarshishBound

"Jonah, Tell us, are you the one to 👉blame👈 for all this trouble😩❓ What do you do 👨‍💼👩‍🌾👨‍🍳❓ Where do you come from🗾❓ What is your country 🇪🇬🇪🇸🇯🇴❓ Who is your tribe👨‍👩‍👧‍👦🚩❓"

Jonah @RunawayProphet

"I am a Jew✡️ from Israel🇮🇱, & I believe🐝🍁 in the Lord, the God of Heaven⛅🌌, who created the 🌊 and the land🌍."

1st Mate @TarshishBound

"OMG 😱! What have you done❓"

Stacy @TheWhyGirl
Why did Jonah run away to begin with?

Mapple @MobyDickPreacher
"As with all sinners among men, the sin of this son of Amittai was in his willful disobedience of the command of God- never mind now what that command was, or how conveyed- which he found a hard command. But all the things that God would have us do are hard for us to do- remember that- and hence, he oftener commands us than endeavors to persuade. And if we obey God, we must disobey ourselves; and it is in this disobeying ourselves, wherein the hardness of obeying God consists."[4]

Dr. King @IHaveADream
"One of the strange facts of human life is the fact that there is within every man an underlying urge to escape God. This is true not only of the rabid atheist, but also of the devout theist. We may not be aware of this in our conscious minds, but deep down within the hidden chambers of the sub-conscious there is the mad desire to flee from the presence of the Almighty God."[5]

Rupert Reinhold III @TheologyZoe
Jonah actually tells us a little about his reasons in **Chapter 4**. *Many people look down on Jonah for his prejudice and anger against their enemy. Some call out his pride and cowardliness for running away. I wonder if Jonah ran away for the virtue of loving his country, for he knew if Assyria repented, they would become the scourge of Israel and wipe them out.*[6]

Jonah 1:11-12

Narrator @TheDivineWord
(Now, Jonah already said 💬 he was running 🏃 ⏪ away from the Lord) The 🌊 was getting more rough & went from 😠 to 😡. So they asked him:

Captain @TarshishBound
"What should we do to you to make the 🌊 😌 for us ❓ "

Jonah @RunawayProphet

"Pick me 🔼 & throw me into the 🌊, & it will become 😌. I know THIS😫 is all my fault."

Gavin @BibleCampKnowItAll
I think Jonah is really brave here. He is taking responsibility for his actions and wants to sacrifice himself to save the lives of the sailors.

Rupert Reinhold III @TheologyZoe
Or he doesn't care for anyone else but himself and would rather die than see Nineveh repent.

How would you describe the character of Jonah based on his actions?

What do you think? Post about it:
#JonahCharacter

Login: Facebook; Instagram; Twitter

Jonah 1:13-16

Narrator @TheDivineWord

Instead, the sailors tried to row 🚣 ⬅️BACK to land. But they could not, for the 🌊 grew wilder from 😠 to 🤬. So, they 📞d out to Jonah's God:

2nd Mate @TarshishBound

"O Lord, please do not let us die 💀 for killing this innocent 😇 man. You, O Lord, are God; You do as you please; You do what is good 👍 & fair."

 **Narrator** @TheDivineWord

Then they took Jonah & threw him out of the 🛥️, & the 😤🌊 became a 😌🌊 right away. This 🤯 of the sailors. They revered ℹ️ the Lord, offered a sacrifice 🐑⚔️, & made vows ✋📖 to the Lord, the God of Israel 🇮🇱.

 **Gavin** @BibleCampKnowItAll
So the God of the Universe answered the prayer the sailors offered up to their own little gods, proving He was better than them?

 **Jarrod** @LittleBirdBible
Yes, but it also looks pretty bad that these non-Jewish sailors appear more righteous than the prophet of God that caused the calamity to begin with.

 **Prof. Rosenbaum** @HebrewScholar7
*The plight of the sailors in many ways parallels the maritime story shared in **Psalm 107:23-32**. I think the point of the story is to show how far the hand of the Almighty can reach to accomplish His purposes. Jonah should have known **Psalm 139**. There is no place on this earth, above it, or under it where one can go where God is not.*

Jonah 1:17

 **Narrator** @TheDivineWord

But the Lord provided a great fish 🐋 to swallow Jonah, & Jonah was inside the 🐋 for 3️⃣ days 🌅 and 3️⃣ nights 🌃.

Stacy @TheWhyGirl
Why didn't they just turn the ship around? That might have stopped the storm, too. Why not throw him an oar to float on along with the cargo since they were not apparently too far from the shore?

St. Cyril @TheAlexandrianBishop
*Jonah was a "type of Christ," to whom our Lord related (**Matthew 16:4**). He descended into the dead and prayed from the belly of a whale. Without the whale, we not only lose the drama of this story but the cornerstone of the resurrection itself.*[7]

Chapter 1: Condensed

God 💬, "Get 🔼 & go to Nineveh," but Jonah 🏃‍♂️⏪ away; God made the 🌊😨; the crew 😱, 🎲🎲, 🙏 d, & threw Jonah overboard; the 🌊 grew 😌. God sent a 🐋 to save him.

Chapter 1 Reflection & Discussion

Whether you are reading as an individual or studying as a group, take some time to explore what is going on in the text and within yourself:

1. When has somebody in authority asked you to do something you really did not want to do? What did you do? *(Verse 1:3)*

   _____
   _____
   _____
   _____
   _____

2. In your life, in your faith, or in the Bible, has God asked you to do something you didn't want to do? *(Verse 1:3)*

   _____
   _____
   _____
   _____
   _____

3. When have you ran away from something or someone? How did it resolve? *(Verse 1:3)*

   _____
   _____
   _____
   _____
   _____

4. Jonah bought a ticket and paid the fare to get to a destination where he never arrived. When have you invested your time and/or money in a dead-end endeavor that never took off or went anyplace? *(Verse 1:3)*

_____

_____

_____

_____

_____

5. The captain asks Jonah to pray to his god to save them, but Jonah doesn't; it seems like he doesn't want to be saved. Is there a time that someone has asked you to pray and you refused? *(Verse 1:6)*

_____

_____

_____

_____

_____

6. Read **Psalm 94:8–11** and **Jeremiah 23:23–24**. Do you believe God knows the hearts of all people? (Why or Why not?) *(Verse 1:14)*

_____

_____

_____

_____

_____

7. If actions speak louder than words, do you think this is true of Jonah? Do your actions speak louder than your words?

_____
_____
_____
_____

Other thoughts, musings, and doodles:

_____
_____
_____
_____

Say a prayer:
*for those you may have refused to pray for in the past.
*that your actions and words are consistent and godly.

Chapter 2
Chapter Breakdown

Verses 2:1-5

Jonah finally speaks to God. In a prayer, which is in the form of a psalm, Jonah vividly describes his desperation and despair as he faces the end of his life sinking to the bottom of the sea.

Verses 2:6-7

Midway through verse six, after exploring the hopelessness and sheer certainty of his own demise, Jonah changes the tone of his prayer into a song of thanksgiving to God for saving him.

Verses 2:8-9

In response to his second chance on life, Jonah reiterates his intention to do what is right.

Verse 2:10

Jonah is redeemed and his deliverance is complete when God commands the great fish to vomit him up on dry land.

Chapter 2 Emoji Lexicon

The sequential usage & definitions of non-literal emoji concepts

Jonah 2:1-3

🙏=Pray

📞=Call

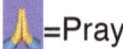=Grave

👂🎧=Listen

🌊=Sea

🌀=Swirl

🌊👋=Wave

Jonah 2:4-5

🥾➡️=Kick

🙈=(Unseen)

⬅️👀=Look

🔁=Again/Repeat

🏛️=Temple

⤵️🚽=Down the toilet

Jonah 2:6-7

🌹➡️=Ebbing away

🎈⬆️=Float

Jonah 2:8-9

✊=Cling

🗿=Idol

🗑️=Waste

🙌=Blessing

📃🎼=Song

🐑🗡️=Sacrifice

✋📖=Vow

👍=Good

👍😇🔒🏆=Salvation

Jonah 2:10

💬👉❗=Command

The Book of Jonah
Chapter 2 & Comment Threads

Jonah 2:1

Narrator @TheDivineWord
From inside the 🐋, Jonah prayed 🙏 to the Lord his God and said 💬:

Mr. Practical @GetRealRadio
Stop right there. The whole premise of a man being swallowed by a whale is ridiculous. How could anyone survive such an ordeal?

Prof. Storia @HistoryIsLife
Actually, history confirms two such cases: In 1771, Marshall Jenkins, was swallowed alive by a sperm whale and survived. While in 1891, James Bartley was found alive but unconscious in the stomach of a whale who swallowed him during a harpooning incident a day earlier.[8]

Mr. Practical @GetRealRadio
And I suppose the Little Bird Bible has a resident Marine Biologist on staff to confirm such sizable whales live in the Mediterranean?

Jenn @SeaLifeAquatic
Actually, currently there are at least four different species of whale who live in the Northwest region of the Sea, including Fin Whales and Sperm Whales.[9] *In fact, bones recently found off the coast of Spain show Grey Whales and Right Whales lived in the region during Roman Times, and possibly Orcas.*[10]

Mr. Practical @GetRealRadio
Oh, Come on!

Jonah 2:2-3

Jonah @RunawayProphet
In my distress 😫, I 📞d to the Lord,
& He answered me.
From the belly of the grave , I 📞d for help,
& You listened 👂 🎧 to my cry 😢.

>
> ***Jesus*** *@LivingWater&Life*
> *"Like Jonah was in the belly of a great fish for three days and three nights, so will the Human One be in the heart of the Earth for three days and three nights."* **(Matthew 12:40)**

Jonah @RunawayProphet
You threw me into the 🌊,
into the very ❤️ of the 🌊,
& the currents swirled 🌀 around me;
wave 🌊👋 after 🌊👋 swept over me.

>
> ***Stacy*** *@TheWhyGirl*
> *Wait a minute; wasn't it Jonah's idea that the sailors throw him into the sea, and here he claims that it was God who did it?*

>
> ***Solomon*** *@TheWisestManEver*
> *"The simple-minded man blames the Divine for the folly of his own shortcomings."*
> **(Proverbs 19:3)**

>
> ***Shakespeare*** *@TheGreatestBardEver*
> *"Alas the frailty is to blame, not we. For such as we are made of, such we be."*[11]

Jonah 2:4-5

Jonah @RunawayProphet

I said, 'I have been kicked 🥾 ➡️ out of Your sight 🙈;

How can I look ⬅️ 👀 again 🔄 upon your Holy Temple 🛕?'

the water of the 🌊 trapped me;
I could not 🤿;
seaweed wrapped 🐙 around my head;
my life was ⬇️ 🚽.

>
>
> **Prof. Rosenbaum** @HebrewScholar7
> *I am pretty sure that the Hebrew word for toilet was not used in the original 7th Century BC text.*
>
>
>
> **Jarrod** @LittleBirdBible
> *Yes, but remember this is a Dynamic Equivalent Translation, which tries to capture the thoughts and feelings of the text more than the actual literal words.*

Jonah 2:6-7

Jonah @RunawayProphet

⬇️ to the roots of the ⛰️ I sank like an ⚓;
the ▪️ to the Underworld was closing on me forever,
but You brought my life ⬆️ from the grave ,
O Lord my God.

When I felt like my life was ebbing away 🌹➡️🥀,
I remembered ☝️ You, Lord,
& my prayer 🙏 floated 🎈⬆️ to You,
to Your Holy Heavenly Temple 🏛️.

Prof. Rosenbaum @HebrewScholar7
*For being in a totally unique situation unlike anyone else in the Bible, much of what he prays is not unique. Nearly every verse is taken from one or more of the Psalms: **Psalms 120:1, 18:4-5, 88:6-7, 5:7, 69:1-2, 49:15, 31:6, 107:22.***

Gavin @BibleCampKnowItAll
When I'm afraid, I say prayers I know by heart like the "Our Father" and "the Hail Mary." Maybe Jonah did, too?

Jonah 2:8-9

Jonah @RunawayProphet
Those who cling 🧗✊ to worthless idols 🗿
waste 🗑️ the blessing 🙌 that they could gain.

But I, with a song 🎼 of thanksgiving 😌,
I will worship & make sacrifices 🐑🗡️ to You.
I have made a vow ✋📖, & I will make it good 👍.
Salvation 👍😇🔒🏆 comes from the Lord.

24

Jarrod @LittleBirdBible
For the longest time, I thought of Jonah being in the whale for three days as a punishment where God put Jonah in time-out to cool off and reconsider his plans. That might be true, but it also might be an additional means of grace that the whale transported him back to where he needed to go (again).

Dr. Hunter @DailyBibleStudyTips
Or, since the book is a satirical parable, it could just be a convenient and amusing way to get Jonah back to Nineveh, which we take much too seriously.

Jenn @SeaLifeAquatic
Actually, since many whales tend to birth their young near the inlet to the Sea off the coast of Spain, if any whale met Jonah near the middle heading East, and traveled at an average speed of 20mph (32kph, 17kn), it would probably take about three days to reach the coast of Palestine.

Jonah 2:10
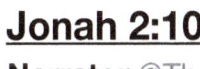

Narrator @TheDivineWord
Then God commanded 💬 👉 ❗ the 🐋 to 🤮 Jonah onto dry land 🏜.

Dr. Lasine @HebrewScriptures&Life
Jonah stands in contrast to many of the heroes in ancient tales like Perseus and Heracles, who bravely allow themselves to be swallowed in order to kill the beast from the inside; there is no need for heroic action here; this big fish is not threatening anyone, including Jonah, so there is no need to fight his way out.[12]

Mother Teresa @MissionCalcutta
"When you have nothing left but God, you have more than enough to start over again."[13]

Stacy @TheWhyGirl
Did he even repent? At no point in his prayer, do I see him say that he was sorry or accept that he did any wrong in running away.

Dr. Hunter @DailyBibleStudyTips
I am with Stacey on this one, because being forced to do something is not the same as changing your mind."

Jesus @LivingWater&Life
"There was a man with two sons; he asked the first son to go work his vineyard. 'I will not,' he said, but later he changed his mind and did. The man asked the second son to do the same thing. 'I will!' he said, but he then did not go at all. Now, which son did the will of the Father?"
(Matthew 21:28-31)

Chapter 2: Condensed
Jonah 🙏d to God: "Sinking like an ⚓, I 📞d for help; my life was 🌹➡️💐 & ⬇️🚽, but You 👂🎧d & saved me. I will make 👍 on my ✋📖." Then the 🐳 🤮d Jonah onto dry 🏞️.

Chapter 2 Reflection & Discussion

Whether you are reading as an individual or studying as a group, take some time to explore what is going on in the text and within yourself:

1. The prayer of Jonah has baffled many scholars over the centuries for though the text says he prayed this in the belly of the whale, the prayer, itself, is written in the past tense and makes no mention of the whale—just sinking and almost drowning. Read the Chapter 2 text again and ask, was Jonah even conscious of being in a whale? What do you think? *(Verses 2:2-9)*

   _____
   _____
   _____
   _____

2. Do you think Jonah repents?

   _____
   _____
   _____
   _____

3. The author of the book of Hebrews discusses how God corrects and disciplines those that he loves, **Hebrews 12:5–11.** Do you think Jonah is being punished for running away?

   _____
   _____
   _____
   _____

4. Is there a difference between discipline and punishment?
___
___
___

5. Is there a time that you have felt God was disciplining you?
___
___
___
___

6. For all the lip service our culture gives to the metaphoric "belly of a whale" experience of sink or swim, nearly dying, and being reborn, Jonah says very little about it and in many ways seems unchanged by the ordeal. Do you think Jonah changed?
___
___
___
___

7. Have you ever had a metaphoric "belly of a whale," sink or swim, nearly dying, and being reborn experience? How were you changed by it?
___
___
___
___

Other thoughts, musings, and doodles:

_____
_____
_____
_____
_____
_____

Say a prayer:
*for God to reveal to you places where you need correction.
*for those you sense are "in the belly of the whale" right now.

Chapter 3
Chapter Breakdown

Verses 3:1-4
Following the big fish incident, Jonah hears God call on him a second time to preach against Nineveh; this time he goes and tells the people to repent or be destroyed.

Verses 3:5-6
A grass-roots movement of repentance begins within the city as the people of Nineveh listen to Jonah, declare a fast, and put on sackcloth to show they are sorry.

Verses 3:7-9
The King of Nineveh catches wind of the repentance movement, tears his clothes, and sends out a proclamation commanding every person and every animal to put on sackcloth plus also to refrain from eating and drinking in hopes of pleasing God in order to avoid destruction.

Verse 3:10
God sees the full extent of the city's repentance and relents from bringing the disaster Jonah promised.

Chapter 3 Emoji Lexicon
The sequential usage & definitions of non-literal emoji concepts

Jonah 3:1-4
😇🧑‍🏫📢=Prophet
🏙️🏛️🏫=City
📞=Call
👣💼=Travel
🔑=of Key Importance
💥=Day
📢=Preach
👎🔥💀🗑️=Destroy, Destruction

Jonah 3:5-6
👨‍👩‍👧‍👦=People
🐝🍁=Believe
💰🍖...🎮=Many Possessions
➡️👂=Heard
💵=News
👘=Robe
🔼=Sent, Send
🪢📜=Royal Proclamation

Jonah 3:7-9
🐄,🐎,...🐔=Animals
🍪🍗🥕🥖=Food
🚰🥤☕🥃🍼=Drinks
👿=Wicked
⚔️🔫⚔️💣=Violent/Violence
💖=Compassion
🔄=Turn
💀=Die

Jonah 3:10
⬅️👀=Look, Saw

The Book of Jonah
Chapter 3 & Comment Threads

Jonah 3:1-4

Narrator @TheDivineWord

Then the Lord spoke 💬 His message to Jonah the prophet 😇🧑‍💼📢 a second time:

God @TheLivingPresence777

"Get ⬆️ & go to the great city 🏬🏨🏢 of Nineveh (NIN-uh-vuh) & 📞 out against it 😫 the message I give you."

Narrator @TheDivineWord

This time, Jonah obeyed the Lord & traveled 👣💼 to Nineveh. Now Nineveh was a very 🔑 city—it was so big, it took 3️⃣ days 🌅 to cross it. On the first day 🌅, Jonah started into the city. He preached 📢:

Jonah @RunawayProphet

"4️⃣0️⃣ more days 🌅 & Nineveh will be destroyed 👎🔥💀🗑️."

>
> **Jeremiah** @TheWeepingProphet
> *That was it? My message or repentance to my own people lasted over 40 years and was 52 chapters long, and Jonah's message to a foreign people was only five Hebrew words long and lasted only three days? Wow, Jonah,*

you got it so easy; no wonder you are a minor prophet.

Dr. Hunter @DailyBibleStudyTips
Ha! Good one, Jerry.

Shakespeare @TheGreatestBardEver
"Brevity is the soul of wit."[14]

Jonah @RunawayProphet
Look, blame God. He specifically told me to deliver only the message He gave me to say.

Dietrich Bonhoeffer @SaveTheChurch
"The first minutes of the pulpit are the most favorable, so do not waste them with generalities but confront the congregation right off with the core of the matter… A truly evangelical sermon must be like offering a child a fine red apple or offering a thirsty man a cool glass of water and then saying: Do you want it?"[15]

Jeremiah @TheWeepingProphet
I really don't think Jonah wanted to offer the Ninevites an apple.

Jonah 3:5-6

Narrator @TheDivineWord
The people 👨‍👩‍👧 👨‍👩‍👧‍👦 👩‍👧 👩‍👦 of Nineveh believed 🐝🍁 God. They declared a fast, & ALL of them, from people with everything (💰🍖🎓🍷📱🦄💍😎🎮) to the people who had 🚫thing, put on sackcloth.

When the 👑 of Nineveh heard➡️👂 this news🗞️, he got ⬆️ from his 💺, took off his royal robe👕, dressed himself in sackcloth, & sat ⬇️ in the dust. Then he sent📤 out a proclamation✒️📜 to the whole city:

Stacy @TheWhyGirl
What is sackcloth?

Prof. Storia @HistoryIsLife
Wearing sackcloth was an outward sign of repentance back then. Sackcloth was literally a heavy coarse material made from animal skin used to make sacks like burlap; it was black in color, hot and uncomfortable to wear, and probably itchy.

Job @God'sFavorite
Tell me about it! (**Job 16:15**)

Prof. Storia @HistoryIsLife
Sprinkling ashes and dust is another outward sign of humility and repentance. Christians keep this trend alive each year to mark the season of Lent on Ash Wednesday.

How do you show outwardly you have repented or turned over a new leaf?

What do you think? Post about it:
#NewLeaf

Login: Facebook; Instagram; Twitter

Jonah 3:7-9

King of Nineveh @TheKingOfNineveh

"By proclamation 🔱📜 of the 🤴 & his nobles: Do not let any 👨, 👱‍♀️, & 👧, or any 🐎, 🐴, 🐄, 🐪, 🐑, 🐐, 🐕, 🐈, & 🐓, taste anything; they shall have 🚫:🍲🍗🥕🥖 and 🚫:🚰🥤☕🥃🍼. But let every 👨, 👱‍♀️, 👧, 🐎, 🐴, 🐄, 🐪, 🐑, 🐐, 🐕, 🐈, 🐓 be covered with sackcloth.

Stacy @TheWhyGirl
Why put sackcloth on the animals? That is really silly.

Prof. Storia @HistoryIsLife
It might seem silly to us, but not to the mindset of the ancients. If the gods were angry, you could put on sackcloth to show you were sorry, but your neighbor could dress their whole family in sackcloth to show they were more sorry. And so it goes...to show the full extent of their repentance, they would even dress their animals in sackcloth out of desperation not humor.

Jesus @LivingWater&Life
"On Judgment Day, even the people of Nineveh will rise up and condemn this generation; for they changed their hearts when they heard Jonah preach; now a greater preacher than Jonah is here, and you won't repent." **(Matthew 12:41)**.

King of Nineveh @TheKingOfNineveh

Let everyone 📞 urgently on God. Let them give ⬆️ their wicked 👿 ways & their violence 🗡️🔫⚔️💣.

36

Who knows ❓ God may yet relent. With compassion 💖, He may turn 🔄 from His fierce 😡 so that we will not die 💀."

Mr. Practical @GetRealRadio
Why would a pagan king give a hoot what the prophet of a foreign god of an enemy nation thinks? This king is not even given a name.

Luther @95Thesis
"Yea, it sounds like a lie, and more extravagant than any fable of the poets; and if it did not stand in the Bible, I should laugh at it as a lie."[16]

Prof. Storia @HistoryIsLife
Actually, scholars and historians have agreed if a foreign prophet's arrival came during the wake of a national emergency, such as an invading army, solar eclipse, earthquake, famine, or flood, the reigning king probably would give a hoot.

Mr. Practical @GetRealRadio
So what?

Prof. Storia @HistoryIsLife
In the tenth year of the Assyrian King Aššur-dān III (773–756), there was a solar eclipse on June 15, 763; an earthquake in the month of Siwan in the reign of an Aššur-dān occurred; there are several references to famine (765-759) or at least recurring famine during these 7 years; plus Babylon was beginning to assert its military might. If Aššur-dān III was king; he probably would have listened to Jonah.[17]

Dr. King @IHaveADream
"Too often have we spent our time arguing over the historicity of Biblical stories, while failing to grasp the underlying truths."[18]

Jonah 3:10

Narrator @TheDivineWord

When God saw ⬅️👀 what they did & how they turned 🔁 from their wicked 👹 ways, He had compassion 💜 & did not send 📤 the destruction 👎🔥💀🗑️ He had threatened.

Stacy @TheWhyGirl
So, did God change his mind, or did he always expect the people of Nineveh would repent? I think he totally changed his mind.

St. Augustine @HippoChurchDoctor
"Being is a name of unchangeableness. For everything that is changed ceases to be what it was and begins to be what it was not. Being is. True being, pure being, genuine being is had only by Him who does not change."[19]

Stacy @TheWhyGirl
Perhaps God's nature and essence didn't change, but God said he would destroy the city, and then he decided not to. How is that not a change of mind?

Rupert Reinhold III @TheologyZoe
This is a question of Conditional vs Unconditional Proclamation. When God says he will destroy Nineveh, that is conditional upon it not repenting, which is why he sent Jonah. If it was an Unconditional Proclamation he would have destroyed it anyway without Jonah.

Pope Gregory the Great @EvangelizeTheEnglish
"He that is immutable changes what He willed,...what changes is a thing and not His counsel."[20]

**Moses** @TheLawBeWithYou

*The true question is did God Relent or Repent of bringing destruction? This came up earlier in **Exodus 32:14**. The Hebrew word* יִנָּחֶם *is the same, but translators debate how to interpret it since the idea of God "repenting" suggests He did something wrong.*

What do you think? Post about it:
#RelentOrRepent

Login: Facebook; Instagram; Twitter

Chapter 3: Condensed

God 💬, Jonah 👣💼d & 📢d, "Repent or be 👎🔥☠️🗑️d." Everyone 🐝🍁d God; the 🤴📬 a 🔍📜 that every 👱‍♂️,👩,👧,🐎🐐🐪🐑🐕, 🐈, & 🐔 should fast. God 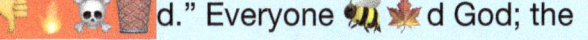👀 this & relented.

Chapter 3 Reflection & Discussion

Whether you are reading as an individual or studying as a group, take some time to explore what is going on in the text and within yourself:

1. History tells us that the Assyrians had a reputation of being excessively violent and cruel as they conquered the surrounding kingdoms and put them under their control. Some have likened sending Jonah to Nineveh, the capital, to sending a Jew alone to Berlin in Nazi Germany in the later 1930's. What is the scariest place you have visited? *(Verse 3:3)*

   _____
   _____
   _____
   _____

2. Who exactly is being given a second chance in the Book of Jonah?

   _____
   _____

3. When have you been given a second chance to redeem yourself?

   _____
   _____
   _____
   _____

4. Jonah's message of repentance—that God gave him to share—is a small part of this chapter being only five Hebrew words long. Why do you think Jonah's message was so short?

_____

_____

_____

5. In **Jeremiah 18:7–10,** the prophet tells us that God can choose to build up or tear down any nation or people. Should this give us hope or fear?

_____

_____

_____

6. The ancients believed in three kinds of gods: personal, family, and national. Both the sailors on the boat of Chapter 1 and the citizens of Nineveh in Chapter 3, start praying to the first set of deities, but end up praying not to the god of their nation, but the God of all creation. When has God revealed himself to be bigger in scope than you initially thought? *(Verse 3:9)*

_____

_____

_____

_____

7. When the Ninevites repented, the Hebrew Bible tells us that they pray to "god;" when the frighted sailors pray, they pray to Yahweh, the personal name for the God of Israel. Does this distinction make a difference?

_____

_____

_____

_____

8. Do you think God can change His mind? Why or Why not? To what extent can our prayers influence divine outcomes?

_____
_____
_____
_____
_____
_____

Other thoughts, musings, and doodles:

_____
_____
_____
_____

<u>**Say a prayer:**</u>
*for those who you do not think know God at all.
*for those who you think need a second chance.

Chapter 4
Chapter Breakdown

Verses 4:1-4
Apparently, Jonah sees the people of Nineveh repenting and loses it; Jonah complains to God about his mercy while explaining that this was the very reason he ran away to begin with. God patiently redirects Jonah by asking him if he has a right to be angry, but Jonah doesn't answer.

Verses 4:5-9
Jonah goes out to watch from a distance if the city will fall. God provides a plant to give Jonah some shade, but then also provides a worm to kill the plant and a hot wind to bring Jonah to the breaking point of discomfort in this object lesson He is creating. When Jonah complains again, God repeats the same question, and Jonah tells God he is justified in his anger.

Verses 4:10-11
God then puts Jonah in his place by reflecting back how Jonah valued the life of a plant over the 120,000 lives in the city he wanted to see destroyed. The book abruptly concludes with a question aimed at the heart of the prophet and the reader about the nature of divine mercy.

Chapter 4 Emoji Lexicon
The sequential usage & definitions of non-literal emoji concepts

Jonah 4:1-4
👹 =Wicked
🙏 =Pray, Prayer
👨‍🎓👉 =Know, Knew
🏃◀️ =Ran
🐌➡️ =Slow
🍾⛲ =Overflow
💗 =Love
📤 =Sent, Send
👎🔥💀🗑️ =Destroy, Destruction
👞🔄🕷️ =Squash like a bug
💀 =Die
📢 =Preach

Jonah 4:5-9
🏢🏫🕰️ =City
⌛⏱️ =Wait
🌱🍇 =Vine
🌱🔃🌳 =Grow
🌅 =Day
🥀 =Wilt
💨 =Wind
💀 =Death

Jonah 4:10-11
🌃 =Night
➡️✋ =Right Hand
✋⬅️ =Left Hand

The Book of Jonah
Chapter 4 & Comment Threads

Jonah 4:1-2

Narrator @TheDivineWord

Jonah, however, flew into a wicked 💩 rage 😡. He prayed 🙏 to the Lord:

>
> **Gavin** @BibleCampKnowItAll
> *Wait, I thought the story ended back in **Chapter 3**. Jonah completes his mission, the people repented, and the city was saved. Why is there more?*
>
>
> **Dr. Hunter** @DailyBibleStudyTips
> *Because that's not what the story is about, so we haven't gotten to the end.*

Jonah @RunawayProphet

"O Lord, before I even left 🏠, I knew 👨‍🎓👉 this would happen; that is why I ran 🏃 ⏪ away as fast as I could for Tarshish (TAHR-sheesh). I know 👨‍🎓👉 of your great grace and mercy. You are slow 🐌 ➡️ to 😠, overflowing 🍾⛲ in love 💗, and eager to stop 🛑 from sending 💨 destruction 👎🔥☠️🗑️."

>
> **John** @TheBelovedDisciple
> *Jonah, God is Love (**1 John 4:8**) He loves everybody. Why are you frustrated or surprised? The Old Testament lays out God's love, compassion, and mercy pretty thick, too:*

(Exodus 34:6-7, Numbers 14:18, Psalm 86:15; 103:8; 145:8, Joel 2:13, Nehemiah 9:17...)

Calvin @GodPredestinedThis
"God preordained, for his own glory and the display of His attributes of mercy and justice, a part of the human race, without any merit of their own, to eternal salvation, and another part, in just punishment of their sin, to eternal damnation."[21]

Dr. Hunter @DailyBibleStudyTips
Which half are you in again, Cal?

John @TheBelovedDisciple
Calvin, you just don't get it; God is Love and Mercy; He is not angry and damning.

Dr. Lasine @HebrewScriptures&Life
God is not angry. In the book of Jonah, it is only Jonah himself who feels anger (4:1,9) One of Jonah's complains about Yahweh's personality is that Yahweh is long to anger (4.2)[22] "Yahweh is not said to get angry when Jonah violates his direct order to go to Nineveh or when Jonah complains and wants to die later on. Nor is God said to be angry at Nineveh."[23] Some scholars suggest we should take Yahweh's wrath and his intended punishments to be functions of the people's situations and attitudes toward him, rather than an indicator of God's own character."[24]

John Wesley @FoundingMethodism
"God, knows every one that does or does not believe, in every age or nation. Yet what he knows, whether faith or unbelief, is in nowise caused by his knowledge. Men are as free in

> believing or not believing as if he did not know it at all. Indeed, if man were not free, he could not be accountable either for his thoughts, word, or actions. If he were not free, he would not be capable either of reward or punishment; he would be incapable either of virtue or vice, of being either morally good or bad"[25]

Jonah 4:3-4

Jonah @RunawayProphet

"Now, O Lord, take away my life; 👞🔽🕷! It is better for me to die 💀 than to live if what I preached 📢 won't happen."

God @TheLivingPresence777

"Do you have any right to be 😡 about this ❓"

Prof. Winglethrush @LiteratureIsLife
This great use of irony is hysterically funny; in chapter 2 Jonah praises God for saving his life; now, he pleads with God to take his life. Jonah is all over the map.

Moses @TheLawBeWithYou
*No one knows how hard it is being a prophet; there was a time I also hoped God would kill me (**Numbers 11:15**).*

Elijah @BaalOut
*Agreed. I also wished for God to kill me (**1 Kings 19:4**); but he never did, but then I never experienced death (**2 Kings 2:9-12**).*

Moses @TheLawBeWithYou
Show off.

Jonah 4:5-6

Narrator @TheDivineWord

Jonah went out to a place East of the city 🏙️ where he made a small shelter & sat waiting ⏳⏱️ to see if the destruction 👎🔥💀🗑️ would come.

Then the Lord God provided a vine 🌱🍇 & made it grow 🌱🔼🥦🔼 over Jonah to give him shade ⛱️. He was very 😖🥵, so this helped calm his wicked 👹😠; Jonah felt very 😀😆😌 about the vine 🌱🍇.

Gavin @BibleCampKnowItAll
A grape vine? Why a grape vine? The Bible doesn't specify what kind of a vine it is.

Mr. Emoji @EmojiGuru
There isn't currently an emoji for a vine of any kind, so pairing a plant with a grape implies the author means a vine. In contrast, the author previously used a whale emoji to convey the Hebrew's wording of a "big fish." Neither is an exact translation, but both convey the idea.

St. Jerome @1stOfficialLatinBible
Actually, many older translations called it a "gourd," but when I translated the Bible, I changed it and suggested it was the large leafy

*castor oil plant. That seemed harmless enough, but a riot then broke out in Oea, a city east of Carthage, and St. Augustine unfriended me. Oops; you can't please everyone.*²⁶

Professor Lui @GeographyGuru
*Given that the daily maximum temperature in Mesopotamia is about 110°F, I think any plant of any size would help bring relief.*²⁷ *The species of plant, or even whale, doesn't matter — The point is God provided it to do as He commanded.*

Jonah 4:7-9

Narrator @TheDivineWord
But the next day 🌅, God provided a 🐛, which chewed the vine 🌱🍇 so that it wilted 🥀. Then God provided a scorching 🔥 East wind 💨. As the 🌞 blazed 🔥 ⬇ on Jonah's head 😥, he grew faint 🥴 and wanted to die 💀 :

Jonah @RunawayProphet
"Death 💀 is way better than living 😖!"

God @TheLivingPresence777
"Do you have any right to be 😠 about the vine 🌱🍇 ? "

Jonah @RunawayProphet
"I do! I am 🤬 enough to die 💀 ❗ "

Prof. Rosenbaum @HebrewScholar7
It is ironic that for a book that thematically deals with a lot of death and destruction, the only casualty actually is a little vine, which was given to the prophet to save him from his own evil.

Dr. Lasine @HebrewScriptures&Life
Many scholars describe Yahweh as being like a father who is patiently leading his pouting child toward the recognition that the father's course of action was correct, and that the "child's" anger and sense of moral outrage were inappropriate; I'm not sure, though, that is what is going on here.[28]

Nahum @NinevehH8r
Everyone just needs to give Jonah a little slack. The city of Nineveh was guilty and deserved destruction; I rail specifically against all its evil ways in my own Book, (**Nahum. 2:11–13; 3:1, 19**), *nearly 100 years later. They deserved destruction and Divine wrath.*

Calvin @GodPredestinedThis
That is my point. God ordained the city would be destroyed, and ultimately it was. Many other Old Testament passages refer to Assyria's fall, too (**Isaiah 10:12–19; 14:24–25; 30:31–33; 31:8–9; Ezekiel 32:22–23; Zephaniah 2:13–15; Zechariah 10:11**).[29]

Peter @FishermanToFirstPope
No, the point is that God was merciful and saved them. God had every reason and right to wipe them off the face of the earth in Jonah's lifetime, but didn't. God is patient and doesn't want anyone to perish (**2 Peter 3:9**).

Is there a limit to God's patience?

What do you think? Post about it:
#DivinePatience

Login: Facebook; Instagram; Twitter

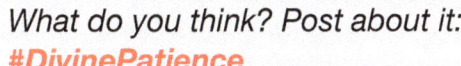

Jonah 4:10–11

God @TheLivingPresence777

"You are 😰 and 😢 about this meager vine 🌱🍇, but you did 🚫 thing to tend it or make it grow 🌱🎣🌳. It sprang ⬆️ over night 🌃 & died 💀 over night 🏙️. But Nineveh has over 1️⃣2️⃣0️⃣,0️⃣0️⃣0️⃣ lost people who cannot tell their right hand ➡️✋ from their left hand ✋⬅️, & many innocent 🐃 as well. Should I not be concerned about that great city 🏙️🏛️🏦⁉️"

Stacy @TheWhyGirl
That's it? How does it end? What kind of cliffhanger season finale of the Sopranos is that?

Dr. Lasine @HebrewScriptures&Life
We leave Jonah when he is still exposed both to the elements and to his God's strange interrogation. He is still allowed no sheltering enclosures and we readers get no closure either. The issues raised by the book remain unresolved.[30]

Professor Storia @HistoryIsLife
Ultimately, it would seem like their repentance did not last very long; Nineveh finally fell in August of 612 BC when the Babylonians conquered Assyria. We guess this happened some 150 years after Jonah's story, unless Jonah was written post-exilic.

Pastor JimmyJay
@UndercoverBaptist
That is the end, though. God made his point through his object lesson; Jonah was undeserving of the shade of the plant God gave him. The people of Nineveh were undeserving of the deliverance God gave them, that they did not fully understand.[31] *That is Grace. If God can come through for even the most unlikable of people and prophets, how should we respond?*

Jesus *@LivingWater&Life*
"Love those you consider enemies and pray for those who treat you badly." (**Matthew 5:44**)

Chapter 4: Condensed
Jonah leaves & ⏳⏱s for 👎🔥☠️🗑. God gives him a 🌱🍇 for ⛱, then a 🐛 to kill it, then a 🔥 East 💨; Jonah is 😖 & 😧. God ❓s why he is petty & 😡 despite His mercy.

Chapter 4 Reflection & Discussion

Whether you are reading as an individual or studying as a group, take some time to explore what is going on in the text and within yourself:

1. Most prophets in the Old Testament share God's message to God's people; Jonah is tasked to share God's message with a foreign people who worship other gods. What does this say about God?

   _____
   _____
   _____

2. Do you think Jonah is more concerned that his enemies were forgiven or that his oracle as a prophet was proven false by God's love?

   _____
   _____
   _____
   _____

3. Do you think God is angry? Why?

   _____
   _____
   _____

4. Like Jonah, have you ever wished God was less loving, less forgiving, or less patient than who He reveals Himself to be?

   _____
   _____
   _____

5. Consider the parable of the Prodigal Son in **Luke 15:11-32**. Are the elements of the Father's love, the elder brother's anger, and prodigal son's repentance similar to or different than the story of Jonah?

_____
_____
_____
_____

6. Some scholars have suggested the book of Jonah is a microcosm allegory of the people of Israel:
   1. God speaks to his own,
   2. His people do not listen,
   3. They are swallowed up by the nations around them,
   4. God goes out of his way to bring them back in-line and give them a second chance,
   5. They botch it.
   What do you think?

_____
_____
_____
_____
_____

7. "Have you any right to be angry?" is repeated twice and is central to the book's theme. Is there something in your life that God may ask of you the same question?

_____
_____
_____
_____

8. Through out the whole book we see God exhorting His power and control over everything in nature great and small from the wind, the waves, the whale, the vine, to the worm, yet He could not control how Jonah or the Ninevites respond to His message. Everything in nature obeys God, except human beings who have the greatest reason to do so. How do you explain this paradox?

_____
_____
_____
_____
_____
_____

9. Other thoughts, musings, and doodles:

_____
_____
_____
_____
_____

<u>Say a prayer:</u>
*for the things you are angry with God about.
*for Peace, Unity, and Contentment.

"The ribs and terrors in the whale,
Arched over me a dismal gloom,
While all God's sun-lit waves rolled by,
And lift me deepening down to doom.
I saw the opening maw of hell,
With endless pains and sorrows there;
Which none but they that feel can tell-
Oh, I was plunging to despair.
In black distress, I called my God,
When I could scarce believe him mine,
He bowed his ear to my complaints-
No more the whale did me confine.
With speed he flew to my relief,
As on a radiant dolphin borne;
Awful, yet bright, as lightning shone
The face of my Deliverer God.
My song for ever shall record
That terrible, that joyful hour;
I give the glory to my God,
His all the mercy and the power."[32]

Jonah in Short

Chapter 1: Condensed

God 💬, "Get ⬆️ & go to Nineveh," but Jonah 🏃⏪ away; God made the 🌊😡; the crew 😱, 🎲🎲, 🙏d, & threw Jonah overboard; the 🌊 grew 😌. God sent a 🐋 to save him.

Chapter 2: Condensed

Jonah 🙏d to God: "Sinking like an ⚓, I 📞d for help; my life was 🌹➡️🙍 & ⬇️🪑, but You 👂🎧d & saved me. I will make 👍 on my ✋📖." Then the 🐋 🤮d Jonah onto dry 🏜️.

Chapter 3: Condensed

God 💬, Jonah 🚶🧳d & 📣d, "Repent or be 👎🔥☠️🗑️d." Everyone 🐝🍁d God; the 👑📤 a 🖊️📜 that every 👨,👩,👱‍♀️,🐄,🐐,🐪,🐑,🐕, 🐈,&🐓 should fast. God ⬅️👀 this & relented.

Chapter 4: Condensed

Jonah leaves & ⏳⏱s for 👎🔥☠️🗑️. God gives him a 🌱🍇 for 🌂, then a 🐛 to kill it, then a 🔥 East 💨; Jonah is 😖 & 😥. God ❓s why he is petty & 😠 despite His mercy

57

Pictorial Character Directory
Cast of characters in alphabetical order

NOTE:
All characters real, historic, or imagined may have no knowledge or concept of the Little Bird Bible
and thus do not endorse it.

The color of the box around the picture indicates their primary category:
1. Royal Blue: Old Testament people.
2. Aqua Blue: New Testament people.
3. Red: Philosophers & Theologians.
4. Green: Inventors & Scientists.
5. Grey: Antagonists & Critics
6. Yellow: Musicians & Artists
7. Purple: Spiritual Beings
8. Brown: Leaders & Experts

A white star indicates the character reflects a generic viewpoint but does not embody an actual person.

1st Mate @TarshishBound. He and the rest of the crew of Jonah's ship chartered for Tarshish were not named and speak collectively. The LBB gave them a name and an icon to make the conversation clearer to read. We know contextually they were not Jewish, and we can assume these sailors were Phoenician.

2nd Mate @TarshishBound. He and the rest of the crew of Jonah's ship chartered for Tarshish were not named and speak collectively. The LBB gave them a name and an icon to make the conversation clearer to read. We know contextually they were not Jewish, and we can assume these sailors were Phoenician.

Adam @TheVeryFirstMan. Adam is said to be the first person God created that uniquely knew God. The story of the myth, the man, and the legend is told in **Genesis 2:4-4:1**. As the story goes, God formed Adam out of dirt, breathed life into him, set him to tend and till the earth within a garden of paradise called Eden. God made him a wife, Eve, and he had everything he wanted, but it wasn't enough; he wanted more, which led him to disobey God's one command by eating forbidden fruit. Many theologians conclude all of life's pain and brokenness proceeds from this original sin.

Calvin @GodPredestinedThis. (1509-1564) John Calvin was a French pastor, theologian, and reformer in Geneva, Switzerland, during the era the Protestant Reformation. He wrote many commentaries on Biblical books, confessional documents, and theological treatises. God's sovereignty and predestination were pivotal foundations of his systematic theology later know as 5 Point Calvinism: 1. Total Depravity, 2. Unconditional Election, 3. Limited Atonement, 4. Irresistible Grace. 5. Perseverance of the Saints. Calvin's greatest single work is *The Institutes of the Christian Religion.* Towards the end of his life, he revised and expanded this great work from 21 chapters to 80. When preaching one of his last sermons, he strained his voice, which brought on a coughing spasm that ruptured a blood vessel in his lungs. He fell ill and died not long after. His body lying in state became a very popular attraction; for fear of a new cult arising, his body was placed in an unmarked grave. The Presbyterian, Reformed, and Congregationalist Churches revere him as a champion of their faith traditions.

Captain @TarshishBound. Captain is in command of Jonah's ship chartered for Tarshish. In the Bible, he is given a voice, but not a name. We know contextually he was not Jewish, and we can assume he was Phoenician like his crew.

 **Dietrich Bonhoeffer** @SaveTheChurch. (1906-1945AD) Bonhoeffer was a German theologian, Lutheran Pastor, and founding member of the Confessing Church. During the Nazi occupation of Germany, he led the underground church teaching pastors secretly in the woods; he was arrested in the conspiracy to kill Hitler, and sent to prison where he wrote his most famous work, *Ethics*. He was executed on the gallows of Flossenbürg Concentration Camp several days before it was liberated.

 **Dr. Hunter** @DailyBibleStudyTips. (1948-Present) Regina Hunter has been studying and teaching biblical content for just over 40 years. She spent two years in Bethel Teacher Training, two weeks at the Bethel workshop to become a trainer of teachers, and at least 30 years teaching Bethel. She has led the St. John's UMC email Bible study since 2007; she plans the studies and selects the scriptures, as well as writing the study tips, which are available free at the website archive at www.daily-bible-study-tips.com and on facebook. She has taken Greek and Hebrew and frequently consults the biblical texts, in addition to commentaries and alternative translations. Most importantly, she tries never, ever to assume that she knows it all. Her Ph.D. is in geology, and her avocation is Lego. In her day job, she was a Distinguished Member of Technical Staff at Sandia National Laboratories.

 **Dr. King** @IHaveADream. (1929-1968AD) Dr. Martin Luther King, Jr. was an American Baptist minister and an outspoken activist during the American Civil Rights Movement from 1954 until his death. His passionate voice for racial equality and practice of non-violent civil disobedience inspired the world and won him the Nobel Peace Prize in 1964. He was assassinated by a gunman in Memphis, TN, while planning a national rally to occupy Washington, D.C.

Dr. Lasine @HebrewScriptures&Life. (1945-Present) Stuart Lasine is an actual professor. He taught Biblical studies, comparative literature, classics, and interdisciplinary humanities for over 50 years, at Wichita State University, The Ohio State University, Western Washington University, the University of Wisconsin-Madison, and the University of Michigan. Dr. Lasine is the author of over forty articles on biblical studies and comparative literature, as well as three books (Knowing Kings: Knowledge, Power, and Narcissism in the Hebrew Bible, Weighing Hearts: Character, Judgment, and the Ethics of Reading the Bible and Jonah and the Human Condition: Life and Death in Yahweh's World). In addition to making scholarly presentations throughout the United States and Europe, he has appeared on the A&E Network and the History Channel.

Einstein @E=MCSquared. (1879 –1955) Albert Einstein was a German-born theoretical physicist known for his theory or relativity. He won the Nobel Prize in 1921 for his contributions to science. Due to his Jewish background, Einstein had to relocate to the U.S. during WWII and helped with the Manhattan Project, though as a pacifist he hated war and was against the use of atomic weapons. While preparing a speech to celebrate Israel's 7th year of nationhood, his abdominal aorta ruptured and he died shortly after at age 76. His brain was removed for study, where it was dissected and parts of it were lost; to date, the last samples to be found were returned in 2013—58 years after his death.

Elijah @BaalOut. Elijah was one of the most powerful prophets of the Hebrew Scriptures, and he is also revered in Islam. He lived in the 9th Century, but we don't know when he was born; he shows up for the first time in **1 Kings 17:1** ready to challenge and call out the evils and shortcomings of Israel's leaders. He goes on to pick fights with the followers of the popular Canaanite god Baal. His stories are epic, supernatural, and legendary. The Bible does not record that Elijah ever died; he was taken up to heaven in a

whirlwind (**2 Kings 2:1-18**). Then 400 years later the prophet Malachi prophesies God will send Elijah back before the Day of the Lord to bring a spirit of reconciliation (**Malachi 4:5-6**), which is why many Jews wondered if either Jesus or John the Baptist were Elijah reborn. Even today, a special place of honor is set at the table in many Jewish homes during the Passover meal in case Elijah returns.

Father Mapple @MobyDickPreacher. A former whaler turned preacher, Father Mapple is a fictional character that gives a stirring sermon about Jonah in chapter nine of Herman Melville's classic work, Moby Dick (1851). The scholarship, analysis, and reflection of Jonah are both passionate and impressive if you read the whole thing.

Gavin @BibleCampKnowItAll. Gavin is 11 years old and has successfully completed every Vacation Bible School in the Tri-State area. He knows the names of all the books of the Bible by heart, along with all the U.S. States and capitals. He represents the young, eager, certain, and sheltered voice of his private Christian suburban upbringing.

God @TheLivingPresence777. God is The LORD God, Almighty, Creator of Heaven and Earth, the Source of all that Is, the Eternal, the Divine Revelation beyond our comprehension, the Living Presence, and over fifty different names given in the Bible. God is. The LBB believes that God is ultimately beyond gender and material form, but in order to see the anthropomorphic emotions attributed to God within the biblical text, the LBB needed to give God a face. Thus, God's face has both masculine and feminine features and is without pigmentation to better convey how God radiates light.

Hellen @OffendedLayPerson. Hellen is the voice of the hard-to-please long-standing members of the local church, who are not afraid to share their grievances and opinions.

Jarrod @LittleBirdBible. Jarrod is the author and creator of the Little Bird Bible. Jarrod occasionally weighs in to clarify the intent and inspiration behind the translation as he strives to simplify and enhance the Bible reading experience. In addition, at times Jarrod shares some of his own scriptural revelations he discovered during his study and translation. His biography is in the back of the book.

Jenn @SeaLifeAquatic. Jenn is the Little Bird Bible's resident marine biologist. While she finishes her undergraduate work, she moonlights as an Orca trainer for a major aquatic theme park.

Jeremiah @TheWeepingProphet. (657-570 BC) Jeremiah is one of the major prophets of the Old Testament. He is credited with writing the Book of Jeremiah, along with the books of 1st Kings & 2nd Kings, and Lamentations along with the help of his scribe and disciple Baruch. He prophesied during the reign of the last five kings of Judah before Babylon conquered Jerusalem in 587 BC and took the Jews into exile. He was known as "the weeping prophet" for his dominant message of judgment that he reluctantly gave. He was ignored, imprisoned, isolated, rejected, and considered a traitor by the religious establishment for advocating surrender to Babylon. Jeremiah continued to prophesy even in exile, where tradition claims he was stoned to death by his fellow countrymen of an exile community in Egypt.

Jesus @LivingWater&Life. Jesus of Nazareth was a 1st Century Jewish rabbi; his disciples believed he was the Messiah and gave him the Greek title "Christ." His life and teachings are best preserved in the New Testament books of **Matthew, Mark, Luke,** and **John.** He was executed on a cross as an insurrectionist and enemy of Rome around 32 AD. People commonly understood that he was a teacher, healer, and prophet, but through his own words and the writings of Holy Scripture, Christians across time believe that he rose again from the dead because he is something more: the Son of God; the second person of the Trinity; the Way, the Truth, and the Life; the manifestation of God's divine love and power in human form; the savior of the world; the redeemer of humanity, and more. We hope you draw your own conclusions through your own reading and study.

Job @God'sFavorite. Job was a holy man who, because of his great righteousness, was put to the ultimate test of faith when he lost everything he possessed and nearly everyone he loved at the same time. In spite of this, he maintained his faith in the Almighty. You can read more about him in the **Book of Job** in the Old Testament.

John @TheBelovedDisciple. John was a fisherman called to be one of the 12 Disciples, who became a missionary and leader of the early church; he wrote the last Gospel, the **Gospel of John**, in addition to the other New Testament books of **1st John, 2nd John, 3rd John.** Some attribute the **Book of Revelation** to him, too. There are over 18 Saints and 23 Popes named John, but the Saint John most people refer to is this one—St John the Evangelist. John often refers to himself as "the disciple Jesus loved" in his own works, and he was the only disciple recorded to be present at the crucifixion of Jesus. John was probably the youngest of the disciples and lived well into old age, but little is known about his

death: **Mark 10:39** suggests he would be martyred, though many believe he was the only Apostle to die of natural causes. Some believe he was buried in Ephesus, others claim he died in exile on the island of Patmos, another 2nd Century source suggests he was boiled alive in oil, but got out unscathed. Perhaps all are true.

John Wesley @FoundingMethodism. (1703-1791) Wesley was an Anglican priest who went on to be the founder of the Methodist Church. Although he had been ordained 13 years before, Wesley had a profound spiritual experience at a bible study on Aldersgate Street in London on May, 24 1738, where he felt his heart "strangely warmed." It was there where his heart took hold of the Gospel, and from age 35 to his death, he saw his life as a mission to preach salvation by faith. He became known for his passionate preaching, which he did wherever he could and often in the fields outside the city limits since he was often forbidden to preach in town. He died of natural causes at home.

Jonah @RunawayProphet. Jonah is one of the few Old Testament prophets sent to prophesy to another people group outside of Israel. Jonah is also the only Old Testament prophet to run away from completing the mission God tasked him to do—prophesying against the capital city of Israel's greatest enemy at the time (Assyria) somewhere between 843-793 BC. Jonah is actually first mentioned in the book of **2 Kings 14:25**, where he prophesies for King Jeroboam II of Israel before the kingdom's fall; we read the rest of Jonah's story in the **Book of Jonah**. Generally speaking, Jonah is often angry and spiteful, but God uses Jonah in spite of himself to accomplish His divine plan, along with other agents of His will from a worm to a whale.

King of Nineveh @TheKingOfNineveh. We know very little about the King of Nineveh who declares a fast in response to Jonah's message. Given the difficulty of pinning down exactly when the book of Jonah was written, that the King of Nineveh was not specifically named, and that this awkward and short-lived episode of repentance was not recorded elsewhere, the LBB gives him a generic place holder name. However, given the historical factors described in Chapter 3, the LBB assumes the king was Aššur-dān III (773–756 BC).

Luther @95Thesis. (1483-1546) Martin Luther was a famous German theologian, priest, professor, hymn writer, and Reformer. Though the embers of the Protestant Reformation had been kindling for some time, Luther stoked the fire in 1517 when he posted his famous _95 Theses_ to the Wittenberg Chapel door on Oct 31; Luther openly challenged and chastised many corruptions and teachings in the Roman Catholic Church. Refusing to recant his teaching, Luther was tried and excommunicated, but he continued to fight back. Luther went on to translate the Bible into the common German language of his countrymen and to found the Lutheran Church. With the fires of religious freedom now raging across Europe, the Protestant Reformation exploded and began to influence many other cultural areas, like education and commerce. He is truly one of the most influential people in Christian history. Luther fell ill in his later years and eventually died of a stroke. His last statement was found on his body written on paper in Latin, "We are beggars."

Mark @TheFirstEvangelist. His full name is John Mark (**Acts 12:12**), and he wrote the first Gospel about the life of Jesus, prior to Matthew, Luke, and John. Mark was a helper and an assistant to the Apostle Peter (**1 Peter 5:13**), where he is thought to have gotten most of his firsthand accounts for his Gospel. Mark was also a traveling companion and fellow missionary of the Apostle Paul on his first missionary journey (**Acts 12:25**). Mark and Barnabas were also cousins (**Colossians 4:10**). Mark was killed doing missionary work in Africa in 68 AD when some of the locals from Alexandria placed a rope around his neck and dragged him through the streets until he was dead. His body and relics were kept in Egypt until 828 when smugglers stole his body, hid it in a cart covered in pork and cabbage to evade detection from the Muslim guards, and sailed back to Venice. San Marco's Basilica was built to bear the saint's name and remains.

Moses @TheLawBeWithYou. Moses lived around 1300 BC. He was one of the greatest prophets of the Old Testament; he led the Exodus out of Egypt and established the Law for the people of Israel. The Bible tells us he was unique and spoke to God face to face (**Exodus 33:11**). Moses led the people out of slavery in Egypt, governed them in the desert for 40 years, and brought them to the edge of the promised land, where he died—never crossing over into it himself. When he died, God himself buried him privately. His grave was never known or marked; some scholars assume this was to keep his tomb from becoming an idol (**Deuteronomy 34:5-6**).

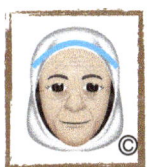

Mother Teresa @MissionCalcutta. (1910-1997) Mother Teresa was born Anjezë Gonxhe Bojaxhiu, in Albania, and became a Roman Catholic nun taking the name Theresa in 1931 from St. Thérèse de Lisieux, the patron saint of missionaries. She started teaching at a school in Calcutta. She was disturbed by the severe poverty of the area and changed focus in the early 1950s to do missionary work with the poorest of the poor. Over the next 40 years her humanitarian work spread across the globe. She opened over 500 missions across 100 counties in her efforts to help people suffering from malnutrition, homelessness, leprosy, tuberculosis, HIV/AIDS, and to help those dying to die with dignity, knowing they were loved. In the Fall of 1997, Mother Teresa died following a series of heart complications. In the Catholic Church, she was later beatified in 2003 and then canonized in 2016 as "St. Teresa of Calcutta."

Mr. Emoji @EmojiGuru. Mr. Emoji is the Little Bird Bible's resident expert on emoji creation and development. He is one of the world's front-running experts on emojis due to his knack for integrating technology, language, and Unicode.

Mr. Practical @GetRealRadio. Mr. Practical is true to his name; he is skeptical of the Bible, organized religion, miracles, and the sightings of the Virgin Mary on breakfast food. Known for his cynical rants on just about anything, Mr. Practical is also the only Little Bird Bible staff member who didn't want the job.

Nahum @NinevehH8r. Nahum is a somewhat mysterious Old Testament prophet. Little is know about Nahum, other than he wrote the **Book of Nahum**, which is the 7th book of the 12 minor prophets. His name means "consoler," and he consoled the people of Judah as he prophesied the destruction of the cities of Nineveh and Thebes. No one is sure when he lived or prophesied and his self-described hometown of Elkosh is also debated. Since the Assyrians conquered Thebes is 663 BC, this is the latest possible date of his writing.

Narrator @TheDivineWord. Much of the Bible is told through an anonymous 3rd person, omniscient story teller who knows the thoughts, feelings, and motivations of the characters in the story, but is at the same time not a part of the story. The Little Bird Bible employs the a Divine Narrator when the authorship of a Biblical text is uncertain, or when it makes it easier to distinguish when the story's main characters move from 3rd person to 1st person in the storyline to speak for themselves. Since we believe all scripture is God-breathed (**2 Timothy 3:16**), it is easier to use an icon of the

Divine Narrator than a generic icon of whatever we think the Holy Spirt looks like.

Pastor Jimmy Jay @UndercoverBaptist. PJJ is the teaching pastor at Mosaic Cobblestone Victory United Family Church of the Very South Valley. The MCVUFCVDV is a nondenominational Millennial multisite church he founded in 2012 outside of Houston, TX, with Baptist roots, Baptist theology, and Baptist polity, but it is not affiliated with the Baptist Church. Pastor Jimmy Jay loves the Lord, his wife, planting churches, and telling his congregation(s) what to think.

Paul @WorstSinnerEver. (?-65 AD) Paul was a distinguished Jewish leader and Pharisee with a brilliant mind and incredible zeal, who started out persecuting Christians before his conversion to the faith. He then became one of their greatest missionaries and authors, credited with writing 13 of the 27 books found in the New Testament, and he still believed that he was one of the worst sinners to have lived (**1Timothy 1:15-16**). Tradition says that after standing trial, Paul was decapitated by orders of Emperor Nero.

Peter @FishermanToFirstPope. (?-68 AD) St. Peter, also known as Simon Peter and Cephas, was a fisherman in Galilee until Jesus called him to follow and be one of his 12 Disciples. Following the resurrection and ascension of Jesus, Peter became a central leader in the early church (**Matthew 16:18**). According to Roman Catholic tradition, Peter was the first Pope; according to Eastern Orthodox tradition, he was the first Patriarch. The books of **1st Peter** and **2nd Peter** are attributed to him. Peter was executed by Emperor Nero in Rome somewhere between 64 and 68 AD. Christian history tells us that Peter felt unworthy to be crucified in the same manner as the Lord, so he requested to be crucified upside-down. He is venerated as a saint in all Christian denominations and also in Islam.

Pope Gregory the Great EvangelizeTheEnglish. (540-604 AD) Gregory was well educated for his day and had a deep inner conflict between seeking personal contemplative holiness and serving the public. He founded several monasteries and reluctantly became Pope (590-604). He was the first Pope to come to power from a monastic background; he was also later recognized as a Doctor of the Church. He was a prolific author and an exceptional administrator whose legacy of powerful civic and spiritual leadership helped align the politics and faith of many of the warring people groups across Europe during the Dark Ages. He was also revered as the Father of Christian Worship for his revisions to the liturgy of worship; Gregorian Chants bear his name. He was lamed by arthritis towards the end of his life, and after his death, he was canonized by popular acclaim and became know as "Saint Gregory the Great."

Prof. Lui @GeographyGuru. Lui is the Little Bird Bible's resident scholar in geography. With her Ph.D. in cartography, she has sailed the seven seas and successfully crossed the Oregon Trail.

Prof. Rosenbaum @HebrewScholar7. Rosenbaum is the Little Bird Bible's resident Hebrew scholar. The etymology of biblical words and phrases are at the center of her teaching and scholarly contributions. Among her peers, Professor Rosenbaum has never lost the Talmud's challenge that during Purim one should drink alcohol until one "cannot distinguish between cursing Haman and blessing Mordecai."

Prof. Storia @HistoryIsLife. Storia is the Little Bird Bible's resident expert on world history. With a double Ph.D. in Western Civ. and a lifelong subscription to National Geographic, she is known for giving the best synopsis of historical periods, people, and places.

Prof. Winglethrush @LiteratureIsLife. Winglethrush is the Little Bird Bible's resident literary scholar. She is an enthusiast of the Classics of Western Literature, and she has a keen eye for English grammar and syntax.

Rupert Reinhold III @TheologyZoe. Reinhold is one of the Little Bird Bible's resident theologians. Endowed with sharp wit and white privilege, his field of study is Hermeneutics, Eschatology, Consubstantiation, which makes him the perfect armchair theologian to pontificate on any subject for any great length of time.

Shakespeare @TheGreatestBardEver. (1564?-1616 AD) William Shakespeare is considered to be one of the greatest communicators of the English language. This famous bard and champion of iambic pentameter is credited with the creation of approximately 39 plays and 154 sonnets. His works have subsequently been translated into most of the world's languages, and his works are performed more frequently than any other playwright. History surmises that he took suddenly ill and died.

Solomon @TheWisestManEver. (990-931 BC) Solomon was the last king of Israel's United Kingdom, which was passed on to him from his father King David. King Solomon is regarded as one of the wisest and one of the richest people to ever have lived, and his reign was a time of great peace for Israel. Solomon is credited with writing

the biblical books of **Proverbs, Song of Songs,** and **Ecclesiastes**. The Bible records that Solomon had 700 wives and 300 concubines, who eventually lead him into idolatry, and there he lost his way (**1 Kings 11:4**). Where Solomon built the First Temple in Jerusalem, it was still smaller than his own palace, and he conscripted slaves to build both. When he died of natural causes around age 60, the kingdom split in two between the Northern Kingdom of Israel and the Southern Kingdom of Judah.

Stacy @TheWhyGirl. Stacy is the voice of Generation Z. Stacy does not identify as religious, greatly distrusts authority structures, and is not satisfied with easy answers. Stacy must always get to the bottom of things. She is not afraid to ask bold or awkward questions to cultivate a deeper understanding.

St. Augustine @HippoChurchDoctor. (354-430AD) Augustine was a Bishop from North Africa and a Doctor of the Church who lived and wrote during the decay of the Roman world. As an ancient philosopher, his contributions greatly influenced Christian teaching and Western thought more than most other thinkers of his era. He grew ill and died during an extended siege by Germanic tribes against his home town of Hippo.

St. Cyril of Alexandria @TheAlexandrianBishop. (376-444 AD) Cyril was an Egyptian-born Patriarch of Alexandria during the height of the city's power and influence under Rome. The fifth century was a difficult time to be a leader in the early Church, as many complicated theological debates took place, and great political rivalries between key cities, Sees, and saints. Cyril was a key architect in developing the belief that Jesus was completely both human and divine without pretending to be one or the other and defending Mary's title as the "mother of God." At the Council of Ephesus (431), he defended these beliefs while preventing a delegation of his political rivals from participating because they showed up late. He was deposed and arrested following the Council for three months; Cyril would not compromise on doctrine, no matter the cost, thus he purged churches of the Nestorian heresy, and evicted the Jews out of Alexandria when the continued religious street fighting with Christians became too much. Apart from sainthood, Cyril is considered one of the Church Fathers (maybe an Uncle by some) and a Doctor of the Church. When he died, he had been bishop for 32 years.

St. Jerome 1stOfficialLatinBible. (347-420 AD) St. Jerome was a Catholic priest, scholar, theologian, hermit, and Doctor of the Church. He was a prolific author, writing many commentaries on Christian life and virtue, particularly for women—many of whom funded his work. He spent 20 years traveling around the Roman world from Africa, to Eastern Europe, to Palestine. He was a secretary to Pope Damasus 1, who commissioned him to produce a singular and acceptable Latin Bible in contrast to the many different texts in use at the time. Thus, Jerome updated portions of the Latin New Testament and Wisdom books. Jerome found the Greek Septuagint Old Testament version unsatisfactory, so he spent most of the rest of his life translating the Old Testament into Latin from Hebrew instead. Jerome's Latin Bible became known as the "Vulgate," for it was written in the common "vulgar" language. Over time, and with a few minor revisions, St. Clement VIII made the Vulgate the exclusive and authoritative Bible of the Roman Catholic Church in 1592. St. Jerome died of natural causes near Bethlehem; prior to his death, he spent several years living in the cave thought to have been the birthplace of a Jesus.

Endnotes

1. Wiersbe, Warren W. Wiersbe's Expository Outlines on the Old Testament. Victor Books, 1993, p. Jon.
2. Melville, Herman. Moby Dick. London, England, 1851. https://etc.usf.edu/lit2go/42/moby-dick/634/chapter-9-the-sermon/ Dec 15, 2022.
3. Einstein, Albert. Letter to Max Born (1926), Irene Born (translator), *The Born-Einstein Letters*, Walker and Company, New York,1971.
4. Melville, loc. cit.
5. King, Martin Luther, Jr., "Fleeing from God." *Stanford University,* King Institute, www.kinginstitute.stanford.edu/king-papers/documents/fleeing-god. Dec 15, 2022.
6. Smith, Billy K., and Franklin S. Page. Amos, Obadiah, Jonah. Broadman & Holman Publishers, 1995, p. 228.
7. Cyril of Jerusalem. "The Catechetical Lectures of S. Cyril, Archbishop of Jerusalem." S. Cyril of Jerusalem, S. Gregory Nazianzen, edited by Philip Schaff and Henry Wace, translated by R. W. Church and Edwin Hamilton Gifford, vol. 7, Christian Literature Company, 1894, p. 99.
8. Stewart, Don "Was Jonah Swallowed by a Whale?," Blue Letter Bible. https://www.blueletterbible.org/faq/don_stewart/don_stewart_629.cfm. Dec 15, 2022.
9. Tethys Research Institute. "Eight different species of whales and dolphins live in the Pelagos Sanctuary in the north-western Mediterranean." *Tethys,* www.whalesanddolphins.tethys.org/cetacean-sanctuary-research/csr-research/. Dec 15, 2022.
10. Hickok, Kimberly. "Pliny the Elder Wasn't Crazy After All. There Were Whales in the Mediterranean." *Live Science,* Future US, Inc., July 11, 2018, www.livescience.com/63028-pliny-ancient-mediterranean-whales.html
11. Shakespeare, William. *12th Night*. (Act 2, scene 2, lines 29-30)
12. Lasine, Stuart. *Jonah and the Human Condition: Life and Death in Yahweh's World.* T&T Clark, London, 2019. p.94
13. "Mother Teresa." AZQuotes.com. Wind and Fly LTD, 2020. https://www.azquotes.com/quote/452204. Jan 18, 2020.
14. Shakespeare, William. *Hamlet*. (Act 2, scene 2, line 90).

15. Thomas, Shawn. "Bonhoeffer on Preaching" *Shawnthomas.com*, June 23, 2015 https://shawnethomas.com/2015/06/23/bonhoeffer-on-preaching/
16. Luther, Martin. "Luther: The history of Jonah is so monstrous that it is absolutely incredible." *Beggars All Reformation & Apologetics*, November 18, 2016, www.beggarsallreformation.blogspot.com/2007/09/luther-history-of-jonah-is-so-monstrous.html?m=1
17. Stuart, Douglas. Hosea–Jonah. Word, Incorporated, 1987, p. 443.
18. King, Martin Luther, Jr., "The Challenge of the Book of Jonah." *Stanford University,* King Institute. www.kinginstitute.stanford.edu/king-papers/documents/challenge-book-jonah. Dec 15, 2022.
19. Armstrong, Dave. "Church Fathers: God is Immutable, Simple, & Outside of Time." Patheos.com, Patheos, April 16, 2018 www.patheos.com/blogs/davearmstrong/2018/04/church-fathers-god-is-immutable-simple-outside-of-time.html
20. Loc. cit.
21. "John Calvin." AZQuotes.com. Wind and Fly LTD, 2020.. https://www.azquotes.com/quote/45689. Jan 18, 2020.
22. Lasine, op. cit., p. 82
23. Lasine, op. cit., p. 112
24. Lasine, op. cit., p. 111
25. Wesley, John "Wesley's Sermon - Sermon 58." *Godrules.net 1998-2017* http://www.godrules.net/library/wsermons/wsermons58.htm. Dec 15, 2022.
26. Smith, op. cit., p. 278.
27. Loc. cit.
28. Lasine, op. cit., p. 10
29. Johnson, Elliott E. "Nahum." The Bible Knowledge Commentary: An Exposition of the Scriptures, edited by J. F. Walvoord and R. B. Zuck, vol. 1, Victor Books, 1985, p. 1493.
30. Lasine, op. cit., p. 119
31. Smith, op. cit., p. 282
32. Melville, loc. cit.

Author Bio

Jarrod Branson Conyers has been studying and teaching the Bible to both young people and adults for the past 26 years. His passion is innovating new ways to connect people to Holy Scripture. His Bachelor of Arts in Sociology and his Master of Arts in Christian Ministry poured the foundation of his profound interest in understanding culture, technology, exploring the nuance of words current and ancient, and sharing the Good News 👍🗞️. Jarrod lives in Albuquerque, NM, with his wife and children; he enjoys poetry, still life photography, and board games. You can email Jarrod directly at Jarrod@littlebirdbible.com, and you can like and follow the Little Bird Bible on Facebook, Twitter, and Instagram.

What's Next for LBB?

The Little Bird Bible LLC is currently developing the next several books of the Bible in this fun and exciting new format. The LBB plans to eventually release all 66 books of the Bible. The next book released will be the **Book of Mark**, but you can go to www.littlebirdbible.com and vote on the books you want to see expedited to the front of the line. You can also drop us a question to add to our FAQ on our website if you are curious about some aspect of the book you just read.

If you enjoyed this book,
please spread the word about Little Bird:
- Please take time rate the book online.
- Please recommend us on Goodreads.com.
- Please find, follow, and like us on:
  facebook.com/littlebirdbible
  or on Twitter via *Logos@LittleBirdBible*.
- Please continue any of the discussions on social media with the provided hashtag prompts.
- Please subscribe our email list on our website to get news and updates on our new releases.

Thank you for buying our book and supporting our mission to simplify and enhance the Bible reading experience for 21st Century audiences!

*When God's mercy
is too hard to swallow*

www.ingramcontent.com/pod-product-compliance
Lightning Source LLC
Chambersburg PA
CBHW042129100526
44587CB00026B/4228